ESSENTIAL **DK** COMPUTERS

WORD PROCESSING

LETTERS & MAILING

ABOUT THIS BOOK

Letters & Mailing is an easy-to-follow guide to Microsoft's word-processing program, Word. This book is for anyone who has no, or very little, experience of using Word.

WORD'S ESSENTIAL FEATURES, from entering text to using Word's pre-prepared documents, are presented in separate chapters to allow easy understanding of functions and how to carry them out.

Within each chapter, you'll find subsections that also deal with self-contained procedures. These build on previous explanations so your knowledge can be gradually developed through a logical sequence of actions.

The chapters and the subsections use a step-by-step approach. Virtually every step is accompanied by an illustration showing how your screen should look at each stage. The screen images are either full-screen or they focus on an important detail that you'll see on your own screen. If you work through the steps, you'll soon start feeling comfortable that you're learning and making progress.

The book contains several features to help you understand both what is happening on screen and what you need to

By the end of this book, you will be able to produce your own letters using Microsoft Word.

do. A labeled Word window is included to show you where to find the important elements that are used in Word. This is followed by an illustration of the rows of buttons, or "toolbars," at the top of the screen, to help you find your way around these invaluable, but initially perplexing, controls.

Command keys, such as ENTER and CTRL, are shown in these rectangles: Enter⏎ and Ctrl, so that there's no confusion, for example, over whether you should press that key, or type the letters "ctrl." Cross-references are shown in the text as left- or right-hand page icons: ⌐ and ⌐. The page number and the reference are shown at the foot of the page.

In addition to the step-by-step sections of the book, there are also boxes that describe and explain particular features of Word in detail, and tip boxes that provide alternative methods and shortcuts. Finally, at the back of the book, you will find a glossary explaining new terms and a comprehensive index.

ESSENTIAL **DK** COMPUTERS

WORD PROCESSING

LETTERS & MAILING

JOSHUA MOSTAFA

A Dorling Kindersley Book

Dorling Kindersley
LONDON, NEW YORK, DELHI, SYDNEY

Produced for Dorling Kindersley Limited by
Design Revolution, Queens Park Villa,
30 West Drive, Brighton, East Sussex BN2 2GE

EDITORIAL DIRECTOR Ian Whitelaw
SENIOR DESIGNER Andy Ashdown
EDITOR John Watson
DESIGNER Andrew Easton

MANAGING EDITOR Sharon Lucas
SENIOR MANAGING ART EDITOR Derek Coombes
DTP DESIGNER Sonia Charbonnier
PRODUCTION CONTROLLER Wendy Penn

First American Edition, 2000

2 4 6 8 10 9 7 5 3 1

Published in the United States by Dorling Kindersley, Inc.
95 Madison Avenue, New York, New York, 10016

Published in Great Britain by Dorling Kindersley.

A catalog record is available from the Library of Congress.

ISBN 0-7894-5529-3

Color reproduced by First Impressions, London
Printed in Italy by Graphicom

For our complete
catalog visit
www.dk.com

CONTENTS

6 MICROSOFT WORD

12 YOUR FIRST LETTER

22 WORKING WITH TEXT

30 CHANGING THE LAYOUT

36 APPEARANCE

42 STORING YOUR LETTERS

46 PRINTING

50 LET WORD HELP

62 MAIL MERGE

GLOSSARY 70 • INDEX 71 • ACKNOWLEDGMENTS 72

MICROSOFT WORD

Microsoft Word has been around for well over a decade and, with each new release, adds to its reputation as the world's leading word-processing program.

WHAT CAN WORD DO?

The features contained in Word make it one of the most flexible word-processing programs available. Word can be used to write anything from shopping lists to large publications that contain, in addition to the main text, illustrations and graphics, charts, tables and graphs, captions, headers and footers, cross references, footnotes, indexes, and glossaries – all of which are easily managed by Word. Word can check spelling and grammar, check text readability, search and replace text, import data, sort data, perform calculations, and provide templates for many types of documents from memos to Web pages. The comprehensive and versatile design, formatting, and layout options in Word make it ideal for desktop publishing on almost any scale. In short, there's very little that Word cannot do.

WHAT IS A WORD DOCUMENT?

In its simplest form, a Word document is a sequence of characters that exists in a computer's memory. Using Word, a document can be edited, added to, and given a variety of layouts. Once the document has been created, there are a large number of actions that can be carried out, such as saving, printing, or sending the document as an email.

LAUNCHING WORD

Word launches just like any other program running in Windows. With the Windows desktop on screen, you can launch Word as the only program running, or you can run Word alongside other software to exchange data with other applications.

1 LAUNCHING BY THE START MENU

• Place the mouse cursor over the Start button on the Taskbar and click with the left mouse button.
• Move the cursor up the pop-up menu until Programs is highlighted. A submenu of programs appears to the right.
• Move the cursor down the menu to Microsoft Word and left-click again. (If Microsoft Word is missing from the Program menu, it may be under Microsoft Office.)
• The Microsoft Word window opens .

2 LAUNCHING BY A SHORTCUT

• You may already have a Word icon on screen, which is a shortcut to launching Word. If so, double-click on the icon.
• The Microsoft Word window opens .

THE WORD WINDOW

At first, Word's document window may look like a space shuttle computer display. However, you'll soon discover that similar commands and actions are neatly grouped together. This "like-with-like" layout helps you quickly understand where you should be looking on the window for what you want. Click and play while you read this.

THE WORD WINDOW

1 Title bar
2 Menu bar
Contains the main menus.
3 Standard toolbar
Buttons for frequent actions.
4 Formatting toolbar
Main layout options.
5 Tab selector
Clicking selects type of tab.
6 Left-indent buttons
Used to set left indents.
7 Ruler
Displays margins and tabs.
8 Right-indent button
Used to set right indent.
9 Insertion point
Shows where typing appears.
10 Text area
Area for document text.
11 Split box
Creates two text panes.
12 Scroll-up arrow
Moves up the document.
13 Scroll-bar box
Moves text up or down.
14 Vertical scroll bar
Used to move through text.

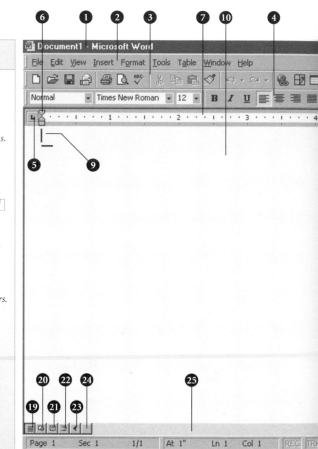

12 Insertion point	**30** Indenting the Address

TOOLBAR LAYOUT

If Word doesn't show the Formatting toolbar below the Standard toolbar, first place the cursor over the Formatting toolbar "handle." When the four-headed arrow appears, (right) hold down the mouse button and "drag" the toolbar into position.

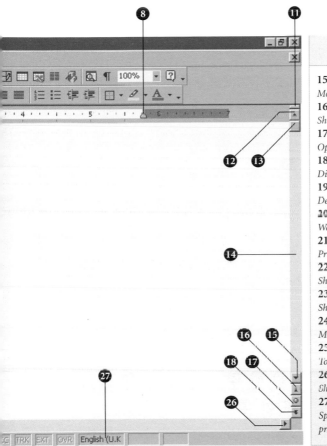

THE WORD WINDOW

15 Scroll-down arrow
Moves down the document.
16 Page-up button
Shows previous page of text.
17 Select browse object
Opens browse options menu.
18 Page-down button
Displays next page of text.
19 Normal view
Default document view.
20 Web layout view
Web-browser page view.
21 Page layout view
Printed-page view of text.
22 Outline view
Shows document's structure.
23 Left-scroll arrow
Shows the text to the left.
24 Scroll-bar box
Moves text horizontally.
25 Horizontal scroll bar
To view wide documents.
26 Right-scroll arrow
Shows the text to the right.
27 Language
Spelling, thesaurus, and proofing settings.

THE WORD TOOLBARS

Word provides a range of toolbars where numerous commands and actions are available. The principal toolbars are the Standard toolbar and the Formatting toolbar, which contain the most frequently used features of Word. There are also more than 20 other toolbars available for display. Click on Tools in the Menu bar, move the cursor down to Customize, and click the mouse button. The Customize dialog box opens. Click the Toolbars tab to view the variety of toolbars available.

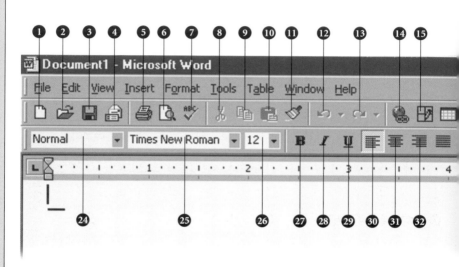

THE STANDARD TOOLBAR

1 New document	9 Copy text	17 Insert Excel worksheet
2 Open folder or file	10 Paste text	18 Columns
3 Save	11 Format painter	19 Drawing toolbar
4 Email	12 Undo action(s)	20 Document map
5 Print	13 Redo action(s)	21 Show/hide formatting marks
6 Print preview	14 Insert hyperlink	22 Zoom view of text
7 Spelling and grammar	15 Tables and borders	23 Microsoft Word help
8 Cut text	16 Insert table	

15 Formatting marks	46 Print Preview	49 Printing quickly

CUSTOMIZING A TOOLBAR

To add a Close button to a toolbar, click on the Commands tab of the Customize box (see left). Place the cursor over the Close icon, hold down the mouse button, drag the icon to the toolbar, and release the mouse button.

ScreenTips

It isn't necessary to memorize all these buttons. Roll the cursor over a button, wait for a second, and a ScreenTip appears telling you the function of the button.

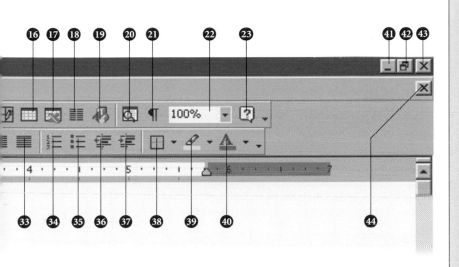

THE FORMATTING TOOLBAR

24 Style selector	32 Right aligned text	40 Font color
25 Font selector	33 Justified text	41 Minimize Word
26 Font size selector	34 Numbered list	42 Restore Word
27 Bold	35 Bulleted list	43 Close Word
28 Italic	36 Decrease indent	44 Close document
29 Underline	37 Increase indent	
30 Left-aligned text	38 Outside border	
31 Centered text	39 Highlight color	

35	Quick ways to align text	36	Font and Font Size	36	Quick ways to format fonts

YOUR FIRST LETTER

Microsoft Word makes the process of writing a letter and printing it out easier than ever. This chapter takes you through the few simple steps involved in creating your first letter.

TYPING THE LETTER

The first image on your screen when you start Microsoft Word is a blank area with a blinking cursor, surrounded by buttons and symbols that may mean nothing to you. Don't worry about them for now. To begin with, the only thing you need to concentrate on is to start writing your letter on that blank screen.

1 BEGINNING TYPING

• Type the first line of your address. As you type, the insertion point moves with your text. Don't worry about mistakes – they are easily corrected ⌐.

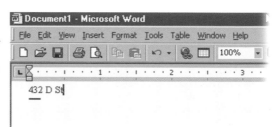

2 STARTING A NEW LINE

• Press the [Enter ↵] button.
• The insertion point has now moved to the beginning of a new line.

Insertion point •

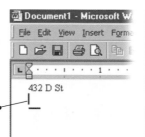

INSERTION POINT

This is a blinking upright line that precedes your text as you type. If you are ever unsure about where your typing will appear on the page, check where the insertion point is.

[14] **Correcting Errors**

3 COMPLETING THE ADDRESS

• Finish typing your address, pressing [Enter ←] at the end of each line.

• At the end of the last address line, press [Enter ←] twice to leave a line space.

```
432 D St
Lincoln
NE 38102

I
```

4 STARTING THE LETTER

• Now type the date, leave another line space, then type the recipient's address.

• Leave two lines (by pressing [Enter ←] three times) and type your greeting.

```
432 D St
Lincoln
NE 38102

August 3 1999

2710 4th Avenue
Omaha
NE 38523

Dear Billy
```

5 CREATING PARAGRAPHS

• Leave another line and start your first paragraph. When typing paragraphs in Word, just keep typing until the end of the paragraph, and only then press [Enter ←]. At the end of each line, Word "wraps" your text round to start a new line.

• To start a new paragraph, press [Enter ←] to end the first paragraph, and press [Enter ←] again to leave a line space. You are ready to start the new paragraph.

```
432 D St
Lincoln
NE 38102

August 3 1999

2710 4th Avenue
Omaha
NE 38523

Dear Billy

It was great to hear from you on Thursday. Good to hear you
much worse than the last place anyway! Hope Rebecca's fee

I
```

6 FINISHING THE LETTER

• If your letter is longer than can fit on the screen, Word moves the text up as you type. If you need to go back to it, simply hold down the ⬆ arrow key. The insertion point moves up the text to the top of your letter.

• Type a farewell after the last paragraph. Press Enter↵ a few times to leave room for your signature. Then type your name.

• You have now typed your first letter using Word.

It was great to hear from you on Thursday. Good to hear y
much worse than the last place anyway! Hope Rebecca's fee

I was speaking to the Jaspers the other day. We really must
gossip. How about our place? We're free next weekend. Giv
think.

Take care

Isaac

| Page 1 | Sec 1 | 1/1 | At 4.8" | Ln 25 | Col 7 |

🏁 Start | 📖 Document1 - Microso... | 🎨 Paint Shop Pro

CORRECTING ERRORS AS YOU TYPE

1 REMOVING THE ERROR

• You have misspelled a word as you are typing.

• To remove the misspelled word, first press the Backspace (← Bksp) key. This removes text one letter at a time to the left of the insertion point.

• Keep tapping ← Bksp until the word is gone.

Dear Billy

It was great to hear from you on Thursday. Good to hear yo
much worse than the last place anyway! Hope Rebecca's fee

I was speaking to the Jaspers the other day. We really must
gossip. How aubot

Dear Billy

It was great to hear from you on Thursday. Good to hear yo
much worse than the last place anyway! Hope Rebecca's fee

I was speaking to the Jaspers the other day. We really must
gossip. How

2 REPLACING THE ERROR

• Now type the word again. Remember to leave a space before it – ← Bksp also removes spaces and line spaces if they are immediately to the left of the insertion point.

• You have corrected the error and you can carry on typing your letter.

Dear Billy

It was great to hear from you on Thursday. Good to hear you much worse than the last place anyway! Hope Rebecca's fee

I was speaking to the Jaspers the other day. We really must gossip. How about|

FORMATTING MARKS

Word uses invisible markers (called formatting marks) within your text to mark the spaces between words, and where you have decided to leave line spaces. Formatting marks do not appear on paper when you print out. Initially you don't see them on your screen,

which makes the text on the screen appear exactly how it will print out. However, you may want to see the formatting marks so that you can see double spaces and control where you want the line spaces to be placed. To see the formatting marks, click on the small, down-arrow button in the middle of your toolbar. A

menu drops down. Click on the button with the paragraph mark. You are now able to see the formatting marks. Click the button again when you want to turn off the formatting marks. You won't need to drop down the menu again – after the first use, Word adds the button to your toolbar.

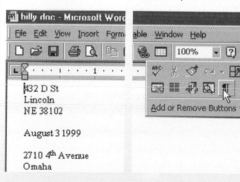

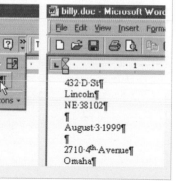

CORRECTING ERRORS FROM EARLIER IN THE TEXT

It is inevitable that errors are made as you type, such as misspellings and duplicate words. If you notice an error higher up in your letter than where you are currently typing, you can move the insertion point back to the error and easily correct it.

1 MOVING TO THE ERROR

• The misspelled word is higher in the text than the insertion point. You may be familiar with using the mouse to relocate the insertion point, but you may be less familiar with using the arrow keys.
• Move the insertion point up to the line containing the error by using the ⬆ arrow key.
• Use the ⬅ and ➡ arrow keys until you've placed the insertion point at the end of the misspelled word.

It was great to hear from you on Thursday. Good to hear you much worse than the last place anyway! Hope Rebecca's fee

I was spaeking to the Jaspers the other day. We really must gossip. How about our place? We're free next weekend. Giv think

It was great to hear from you on Thursday. Good to hear you much worse than the last place anyway! Hope Rebecca's fee

I was spaeking to the Jaspers the other day. We really must gossip. How about our place? We're free next weekend. Giv think.

2 CORRECTING THE ERROR

• Remove the misspelled word and type it in with the correct spelling.
• You have now corrected the error. Use the ⬇ arrow key to return the insertion point to where you left off. You can now continue with your typing.

It was great to hear from you on Thursday. Good to hear you much worse than the last place anyway! Hope Rebecca's fee

I was speaking to the Jaspers the other day. We really must gossip. How about our place? We're free next weekend. Giv think.

ADDING WORDS IN THE MIDDLE OF THE TEXT

Word makes it easy for you to change your text at any time while writing your letter. If you decide to add something further, or suddenly realize that an important point has been left out, you can type it in by first using the insertion point.

1 POSITIONING THE INSERTION POINT

• Move the insertion point to the place in the text where you want to add words. Use the arrow keys on your keyboard again for further practice. Remember, you can only move to where text has already been typed.

Insertion point •

Omaha
NE 38523

Dear Billy

It was great to hear from you on Thursday. Good to hear you much worse than the last place anyway! Hope Rebecca's fee

I was speaking to the Jaspers the other day. We really must gossip. How about our place? We're free next weekend. Giv think.

Take care

Isaac.

2 ADDING THE WORDS

• Start typing the new text. If the insertion point is in the middle of a paragraph, you'll notice that Word automatically moves text along to accommodate what you are adding.
• Use the arrow keys to return to the place where you left off typing.

Omaha
NE 38523

Dear Billy

It was great to hear from you on Thursday. Good to hear you much worse than the last place anyway! Hope Rebecca's fee

I was speaking to the Jaspers the other day. We really must gossip. I can't wait. How about our place? We're free next w what you think.

Take care

MANIPULATING PARAGRAPHS

Paragraphs organize your text, help with the sense of your document, and make your document more readable. With Word it's easy to create a new paragraph when another is needed, and to combine them when two paragraphs aren't required.

1 SPLITTING A PARAGRAPH

• To split a paragraph into two, move the insertion point to the start of the sentence that will begin the new second paragraph. Then press [Enter ←] twice. You now have two paragraphs.

> I was speaking to the Jaspers the other day. We really must a
> gossip. I can't wait! How about our place? We're free next w
> what you think.
>
> Take care

> I was speaking to the Jaspers the other day. We really must a
> gossip. I can't wait!
>
> How about our place? We're free next weekend. Give us a b
>
> Take care

2 COMBINING PARAGRAPHS

• If you want to join two paragraphs together to make one, place the insertion point at the beginning of the second paragraph. Then press [← Bksp] twice to remove the line spaces. Your two paragraphs now form one larger paragraph.

> It was great to hear from you on Thursday. Good to hear you're settling into the new office. It c
> much worse than the last place anyway! Hope Rebecca's feeling better now.
>
> I was speaking to the Jaspers the other day. We really must all meet up and catch up on the last
> gossip. I can't wait! How about our place? We're free next weekend. Give us a bell and let me l
> what you think.
>
> Take care

3 PARAGRAPH MARKS

• Pressing the [Enter ←] key ends a paragraph and inserts a paragraph mark. You can see these marks by turning on the formatting marks ⌐. Deleting the line space between paragraphs is just a matter of deleting the paragraph mark just like any other character.

It was great to hear from you on Thursday. Good to hear you're settling into the new office. It much worse than the last place anyway! Hope Rebecca's feeling better now. I was speaking to Jaspers the other day. We really must all meet up and catch up on the last year's gossip. I can't wait! How about our place? We're free next weekend. Give us a bell and let me know what you

Take care

USING WORD TO START A NEW PAGE

If you want to begin a new page, before the text has reached the end of the current page, you can use Word to split the page into two.

Move the insertion point to the position in your letter where you want the new page to start.
Hold down the [Ctrl] key and press [Enter ←]. Word inserts a "manual" page break. You can delete this page break by placing the insertion point at the top left of the second page and pressing [← Bksp].

Dear Billy

It was great to hear from you on Thursday. Good to hear you're settling into the new office. I much worse than the last place anyway! Hope Rebecca's feeling better now.

I was speaking to the Jaspers the other day. We really must all meet up and catch up on the la gossip. I can't wait! How about our place? We're free next weekend. Give us a bell and let me what you think.

Dear Billy

It was great to hear from you on Thursday. Good to hear you're settling into the new office. I much worse than the last place anyway! Hope Rebecca's feeling better now.
--Page Break--
I was speaking to the Jaspers the other day. We really must all meet up and catch up on the la gossip. I can't wait! How about our place? We're free next weekend. Give us a bell and let me what you think.

---

15 **Formatting marks**

SAVING YOUR LETTER

Now that your letter is finished and correct, you should save it as a file on your computer's hard disk so that if you need to find it later, or make changes after you have printed it out, you will be able to bring it back up on the screen.

1 SAVING THE FILE

• Move your mouse pointer over the word File in the Menu bar at the top of the screen. Click on File and the File menu drops down. Move the mouse pointer down and click on Save.

• The Save As dialog box pops up in the middle of your screen. In this box you are able to give your letter a file name and decide where you want to save it on the hard disk.

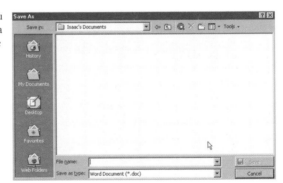

2 NAMING AND SAVING

• Choose a file name that identifies the letter for you and type it into the File name box.

• Select a folder in the Save in box and click on the Save button. The dialog box closes and your letter is saved to disk.

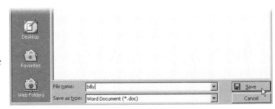

PRINTING YOUR LETTER

1 FILE PRINT

• Click on the File menu. The File menu drops down.
• This time choose Print from the File menu by clicking once on Print.

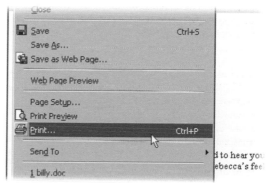

2 PRINT YOUR LETTER

• The Print dialog box pops up. Don't worry about any of the features here at this stage. Just make sure that the printer is plugged into the computer and is switched on.
• Click on the OK button at the bottom of the dialog box and your letter begins to print.

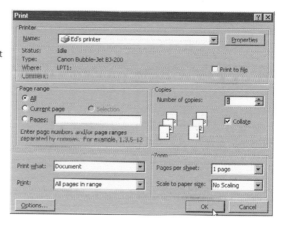

Well done...

You have now typed, corrected, saved, and printed your first letter using Word. These simple steps have shown you the basic process that you use to create a letter with Microsoft Word. Now we go into more detail and explore each step of the process in detail.

WORKING WITH TEXT

This section deals with methods of working with text: moving around text, shifting text from one place to another, deleting text, and copying text.

MOVING AROUND YOUR TEXT

There are many different ways to move around and see different parts of your letter. Here are some techniques to move through your letter that make use of either the mouse or the different actions that are available through the keyboard.

1 GET TO THE START OF THE LETTER

• The insertion point is midway through or at the end of the letter.
• Hold down the [Ctrl] key and press the [Home] key on your keyboard.
• The screen now shows the top of the letter. The insertion point is at the very beginning of the text.

The insertion point moves to the start of the letter

Dear Billy

It was great to hear from you on Thursday. Good to hear you
much worse than the last place anyway! Hope Rebecca's fee

I was speaking to the Jaspers the other day. We really must
gossip. I can't wait! How about our place? We're free next w
what you think.

Take care

---

432 D St
Lincoln
NE 38102

August 3 1999

2710 4th Avenue
Omaha
NE 38523

Dear Billy

2 GET TO THE END OF THE TEXT

- Hold down the Ctrl key and press the End key on your keyboard.
- The screen now shows the foot of the letter. The insertion point is at the very end of the text.

> I was speaking to the Jaspers the other day. We really must ʒ
> gossip. I can't wait! How about our place? We're free next v
> what you think.
>
> Take care
>
>
> Isaac

3 SCROLLING THROUGH TEXT

- If you can't see the part of the letter you want, position the mouse cursor over the sliding box in the scroll bar.

Hold down the left mouse button and move the box up and down the bar to scroll through the text.
- Alternatively, use the buttons at the top and

bottom of the scroll bar. Click on them to scroll the text up and down.
- Stop when the section of the text appears that you want to work on.

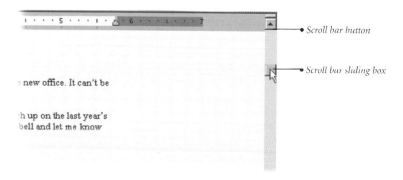

- Scroll bar button
- Scroll bar sliding box

 new office. It can't be

 h up on the last year's
 bell and let me know

MOVING AROUND WITHOUT THE MOUSE

If you want to move quickly around your letter without using the mouse, you can use the PgUp and PgDn keys on your keyboard to move up or down your letter one screen at a time. This method moves the insertion point directly. You can use the arrow keys to place the insertion point in the exact position in the text where you need to make your changes.

4 CLICKING ON TEXT

• Move the mouse pointer to the exact point in the text where you want the insertion point to go.
• Left-click once. The insertion point appears.

Dear Billy

It was great to hear from you on Thursday. Good to hear you much worse than the last place anyway! Hope Rebecca's fee

I was speaking to the Jaspers the other day. We really must gossip. I can't wait! How about our place? We're free next w what you think.

Take care

SELECTING TEXT

Before Word can carry out any changes that you want to make, you first need to tell Word what parts of the text you want it to work on. This is done by selecting text, which is one of the most frequently used operations when using Word.

1 USING THE KEYBOARD

• Move the insertion point to the start of the text you want to select.
• Hold down the ⇧ Shift key and press the → arrow key. This has the effect of creating a block of selected text one letter at a time.

It was great to hear from you on Thursday. Good to hear you much worse than the last place anyway! Hope Rebecca's fee

I was speaking to the Jaspers the other day. We really must gossip. I can't wait! How about our place? We're free next w what you think.

Take care

It was great to hear from you on Thursday. Good to hear you much worse than the last place anyway! Hope Rebecca's fee

I was speaking to the Jaspers the other day. We really must gossip. I can't wait! How about our place? We're free next w what you think.

Take care

• If the block you want to select extends over more than one line, keep the ⟨⇧ Shift⟩ key held down, and press the ⟨↓⟩ key to select whole lines at a time. Then use the ⟨←⟩ and ⟨→⟩ keys to choose the end of the block. Don't release the ⟨⇧ Shift⟩ key until you have selected the entire block of text that you want.

Dear Billy

It was great to hear from you on Thursday. Good to hear you
much worse than the last place anyway! Hope Rebecca's fee

I was speaking to the Jaspers the other day. We really must
gossip. I can't wait! How about our place? We're free next w
what you think.

Take care

Vanishing Point

You will notice that when you have selected and highlighted a block of text, there is no longer an insertion point in your Word window. What has happened is that the block of selected text becomes one very large insertion point. It is important to be careful here because if you press any character key on the keyboard while your block is selected, your entire block will vanish and be replaced by whatever you type.

2 USING THE MOUSE

• Move the mouse pointer to the precise point where you want to start your selected block of text.
• Hold down the left mouse button and move the mouse pointer to the position that marks the end of the block that you want.
• Release the mouse button. Your block of text is now selected.
• If you make a mistake, simply click outside the selection and go through the process again.

Dear Billy

It was great to hear from you on Thursday. Good to hear you
much worse than the last place anyway! Hope Rebecca's fee

I was speaking to the Jaspers the other day. We really must
gossip. I can't wait! How about our place? We're free next w
what you think.

Dear Billy

It was great to hear from you on Thursday. Good to hear you
much worse than the last place anyway! Hope Rebecca's fee

I was speaking to the Jaspers the other day. We really must
gossip. I can't wait! How about our place? We're free next w
what you think.

3 SELECTING ALL THE TEXT

• Click on Edit on the menu bar. The Edit menu drops down.

• Now click on Select All in the Edit menu.

• The whole of your letter is now selected.

• Alternatively, you can move the mouse cursor to the left of your text where it changes from pointing left to pointing to the right. Hold down the [Ctrl] key and click on the left mouse button. The whole of your text is now selected.

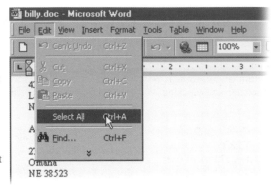

4 SELECTING LINES AT A TIME

Selecting blocks of text by lines can save time. Move the mouse pointer to the left of the first line that you want to select. Hold down the left mouse button and move the mouse pointer to the last line of your chosen block. Release the mouse button and the block is selected.

MOVING TEXT – CUT AND PASTE

You can move whole blocks of text either within your document or between documents when using Word. The easiest way to do this is by "cutting" selected blocks of text from your letter and "pasting" them back into a different place.

1 CUTTING TEXT

- Select a block of text.
- Click on Edit on the menu bar. The Edit menu drops down.
- Click on Cut in the Edit menu. Your block of text will disappear, but it is not lost. The rest of the text will move back into place around it.

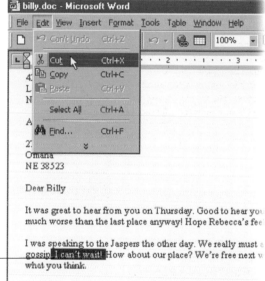

Block of text to be cut

Cutting has removed the text

2 PASTING TEXT

• Position the insertion point where you want the text to reappear.
• Click on Edit in the Menu bar, then on Paste in the drop down menu.
• The text is pasted back into your letter exactly where you want it.

Dear Billy

It was great to hear from you on Thursday. Good to hear you much worse than the last place anyway! Hope Rebecca's fee

I was speaking to the Jaspers the other day. We really must a gossip. How about our place? We're free next weekend. Giv think

Take care

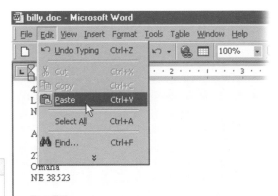

COPYING TEXT

You may want to copy a block of text to a new location while leaving the original block in its old position. Simply go through the cut and paste procedures detailed on these pages, but when you come to cut the text, select Copy instead of Cut on the Edit menu. The block will stay where it is, but you will be able to paste copies of it whenever you want.

Omaha
NE 38523

Dear Billy

It was great to hear from you on Thursday. Good to hear you

Dear Billy

It was great to hear from you on Thursday. Good to hear you much worse than the last place anyway! Hope Rebecca's fee

I was speaking to the Jaspers the other day. We really must a gossip. How about our place? We're free next weekend. Giv think. I can't wait!

Take care

MOVING TEXT – DRAG AND DROP

This method is a quicker way of moving text around and uses only the mouse. Once you've told Word what part of the text you want to move, you can then "drag" it to the position where you want to move it, and "drop" it into place.

1 SELECTING THE TEXT

• Select a block of text using one of the methods that you have already learned ⬚.

Dear Billy

It was great to hear from you on Thursday. Good to hear you much worse than the last place anyway! Hope Rebecca's fee

I was speaking to the Jaspers the other day. We really must a gossip. How about our place? We're free next weekend. Giv think. I can't wait!

Take care

2 MOVING THE TEXT

• Place the mouse cursor over the block of selected text. Hold down the left mouse button and move, or "drag," the mouse cursor to the position in your letter where you want the text to appear. Don't release the mouse button until the mouse pointer is in exactly the right place.
• Now release the mouse button and the text appears in the new location.

Dear Billy

It was great to hear from you on Thursday. Good to hear you much worse than the last place anyway! Hope Rebecca's fee

I was speaking to the Jaspers the other day. We really must a gossip. How about our place? We're free next weekend. Giv think. I can't wait!

Take care

Dear Billy

It was great to hear from you on Thursday. Good to hear you much worse than the last place anyway! Hope Rebecca's fee

I was speaking to the Jaspers the other day. We really must a gossip. We're free next weekend. How about our place? Giv think. I can't wait!

Take care

24 Selecting Text

CHANGING THE LAYOUT

In this section we deal with how to lay your text out on the page in the way you want it. The most common layout changes that you'll be making are indenting and aligning.

INDENTING THE ADDRESS

1 SELECTING YOUR ADDRESS

• Using either the mouse or the keyboard, select the lines of your address as a block of text .

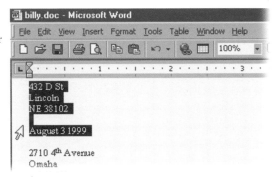

2 CHANGING THE INDENT

• Directly above the text on the screen is a numbered line. This is the ruler.
• Move your mouse pointer to the small symbol called the left indent marker shown at right.
• Click on the box at the base of the left indent marker, and hold down the left mouse button.

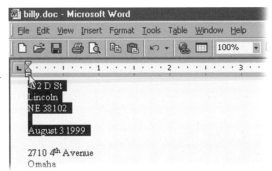

24 **Selecting Text**

• Drag the left indent marker, by using the box, across the ruler however far you want your address to be indented.

• Now release the mouse button. Your address has moved across the screen.

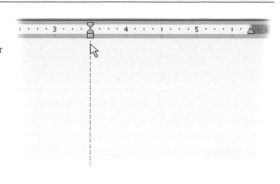

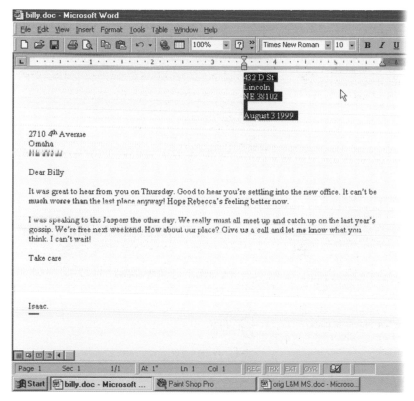

INDENTING PARAGRAPHS

You may want to make each of your paragraphs begin a little further into the page than the main text (a "first line indent"). Or you may want the body of

text indented except for the lines beginning each paragraph (a "hanging indent"). These steps take you through how to do each of these procedures.

1 SELECT THE PARAGRAPHS

• Select only the paragraphs of text in your letter and not the addresses, date, greeting, and sign-off.

2710 4th Avenue
Omaha
NE 38523

Dear Billy

It was great to hear from you on Thursday. Good to hear you
much worse than the last place anyway! Hope Rebecca's fee

I was speaking to the Jaspers the other day. We really must
gossip. We're free next weekend. How about our place? Giv
think. I can't wait!

Take care

2 FIRST LINE INDENT

• Move your mouse pointer over the left indent marker on the ruler.
• When the pointer is on the top part of the left indent marker, hold down the left mouse button.
• Drag the pointer along the ruler to however far in you want the indent.

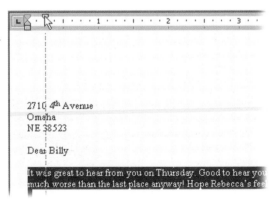

2710 4th Avenue
Omaha
NE 38523

Dear Billy

It was great to hear from you on Thursday. Good to hear you
much worse than the last place anyway! Hope Rebecca's fee

• Release the mouse button. The first lines of each of your paragraphs are now indented.

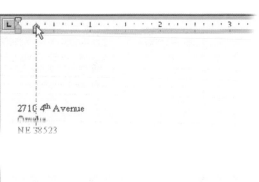

3 HANGING INDENT

• For a hanging indent, go through Step 1 (opposite) to select the text.

• Now, move the mouse pointer until it is over the left indent marker.

• Position the pointer over the middle part of the left indent marker, (avoiding the other two parts of the left indent marker may need some practice).

• Hold down the left mouse button and drag the pointer over to the right as far as you want the paragraphs to be indented.

• Release the mouse button. Your paragraphs are now formatted with a hanging indent.

ALIGNMENT

At the moment all your text except for your address is aligned to the left – the left side is straight while the right is ragged, like text created with a typewriter. Word can make the right side straight as well, like text in a book (this is called "justified text"). Other possibilities include aligning your text to the right, which leaves the left side ragged, or centering the text exactly down the middle of the page.

1 JUSTIFIED TEXT

• Select the text you want to realign.
• Drop down the Format menu from the menu bar at the top of the screen.
• Click on Paragraph in the Format menu and the Paragraph dialog box opens on screen.
• Click on the drop-down button next to the Alignment option. A small menu will drop down.
• Click on the word Justified in this menu.
• Click on OK and the dialog box closes.

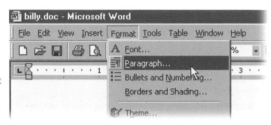

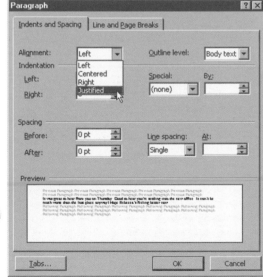

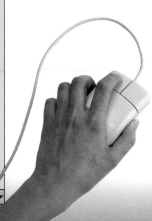

• Your text is now justified with the left- and right-hand sides both straight.

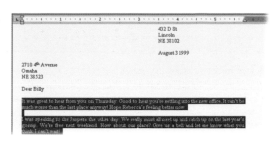

2 RIGHT-ALIGNED TEXT

• Follow Step 1 (opposite) until you get to the Alignment drop-down menu in the Paragraph dialog box.
• This time click on Right and then on OK.
• Your text has been aligned to the right.

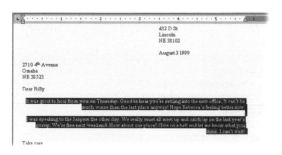

3 CENTERED TEXT

• Follow Step 1 until you get to the Alignment drop-down menu in the Paragraph dialog box.
• Click on Center this time, then on OK.
• Your text has been centered on the page.

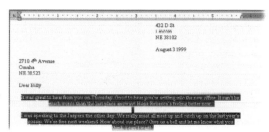

QUICK WAYS TO ALIGN TEXT

 You are also able to realign text by using the alignment buttons (shown at left) on the toolbar at the top of the screen. First select the text and click on the button you need. From left to right, the buttons mean: left-align, center, right-align, and justify.

APPEARANCE

Your letter now looks better than it did before. However, there are many other tweaks and touches that can transform your text to just the way you want it to appear.

FONT AND FONT SIZE

The font is the kind of lettering that Word uses to display your text. You may wish to use different fonts in different kinds of letter: a stern, professional-looking font for business letters, and a lighter, friendlier font for your personal letters. You may also wish either to increase or decrease the size of the font that you use.

1 THE FONT DIALOG BOX

• Select all the text in the document ⬚.
• Drop down the Format menu from the menu bar.
• Choose Font in the Format menu. The Font dialog box opens.

QUICK WAYS TO FORMAT FONTS

B *I* <u>U</u> You may have noticed that the font, font size, and the buttons for bold, italic, and underline are included in the Formatting toolbar (just above the ruler). To format fonts without using the Font dialog box, you can select the text and use these tools to format it. The font and font size are drop-down menus. The font style buttons (shown left) click in or out to show if, say, Bold is on or off in a selected block of text.

---

24 Selecting Text

2 CHANGING THE FONT

• The Font menu is displayed under the Font tab in the Font dialog box. Scroll up and down it using the scroll bar at the side of the menu. Your text is probably in Times New Roman at the moment.

• As you click on different fonts, the appearance of the selected font is shown in the Preview box in the Font dialog box.

• Keep scrolling through the fonts until you find one you want to use.

Preview Box ●

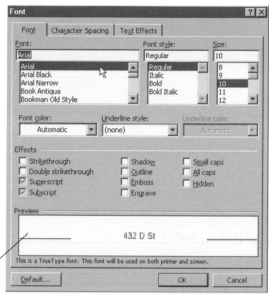

3 FONT SIZE

• Now check the Size menu at top right of the Font dialog box.

• The font size is probably set to 10. This is quite small. Try clicking on 12 or any font size you want – 10 and 12 are the most often used in plain text.

• The Preview box will show the new font in its new size.

4 APPLYING YOUR CHANGES

• When you are satisfied with the font and font size, click on the OK button.
• The Font dialog box will close. Your text is now formatted in the new font and font size.

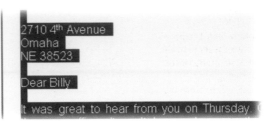

FONT STYLE

In addition to the regular font, there are three other font styles – bold, italic, and underline – that can be used to emphasize individual words, phrases, or any other block of text. They can also be used in combination for extra effect.

1 BOLD TEXT

• Select the text you want to make bold.
• Open the Font dialog box from the Format menu.
• In the Font style menu click on Bold.
• Click OK to close the Font dialog box.
• Your selected text now appears in bold.

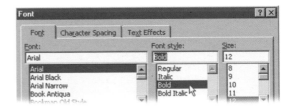

Bold text •———

2 ITALIC TEXT

• Follow Step 1 (opposite), but click on Italic in the Font Style menu of the Font dialog box.

• Click OK to close the Font dialog box.

• Your selected text is now displayed in italics.

Italicized text •

Dear Billy

It was **great** to hear from you on Thursday. (the new office. It can't be much worse tha Rebecca's feeling better now.

I was speaking to the Jaspers the other day catch up on the last year's gossip. We're fre place? Give us a call and let me know what you

Take care

3 UNDERLINED TEXT

• Select the text and open the Font dialog box in the usual way.

• Drop down the Underline menu (below the Font menu in the dialog box).

• There are many underline options, but the most useful is Single – a single line under the selected text. An alternative is Words only – each word is underlined, but not the spaces separating them. Click on your choice.

• Click OK to close the Font dialog box.

• The selection is now emphasized by underlining.

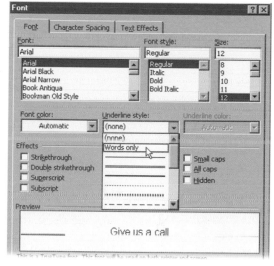

Words only •
underlined text

I was speaking to the Jaspers the other day catch up on the last year's gossip. We're fre place? Give us a call and let me know what you

Take care

LINE SPACING

You may want to increase the spacing between the lines of your letter – some find it easier to read. For example, double line spacing creates a space the height of one line between each line of the text. Other options are also available.

1 SELECT THE ENTIRE LETTER
• Click on Format on the menu bar to drop down the Format menu.
• Click on Paragraph from the Format menu to open the Paragraph dialog box.

2 LINE SPACING SELECTION
• Click the small down arrow on the right of the Line spacing box. The Line spacing menu drops down.
• Choose Double line spacing from the menu.
• Click on the OK button. Your selected text now appears with the chosen line spacing.

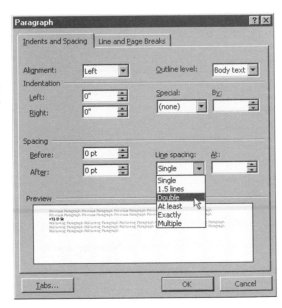

• Click on the OK button. Your selected text now appears with the chosen line spacing.

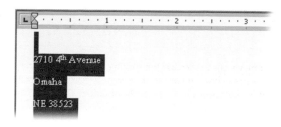

3 MULTIPLE LINE SPACING

You are not limited only to single, 1.5, and double line spacing when using Word.

• Select part of your text and click the down arrow in the Line spacing box. The Line spacing menu drops down.

• Click on Multiple at the foot of the menu.

• In the At: box the figure 3 appears. Three-line spacing is the default selection for multiple line spacing. If you want a different number, highlight the 3, type the number of line spaces, and click on OK.

• The lines of your selected text are now separated by your chosen line spacing.

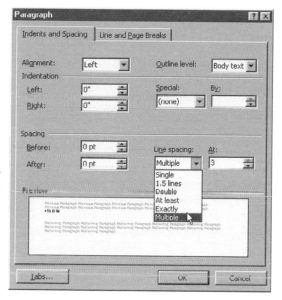

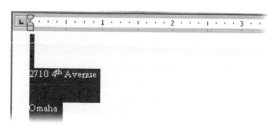

STORING YOUR LETTERS

It is usually essential to save your letters on your hard disk so that you can refer to them at a later date. This section provides an overview of how to store and recall your text.

WORKING WITH FILES

A file is what we call any piece of data that is stored on a computer's hard disk. This could be a spreadsheet, a program, or your letter that you have created using Word. Not only can you store (save) your documents when you have completed them, it is important that you also save your files as you work, especially if they are long and you have put a lot of work into them. If your computer suddenly crashes you could lose everything you have done since you last saved your work.

1 CREATING A NEW FILE
• When you open Word, a new file is automatically created in which you can begin typing.
• You may want to create other new files later on. Drop down the File menu and click on New.
• Click on Blank Document to select it and click on OK.

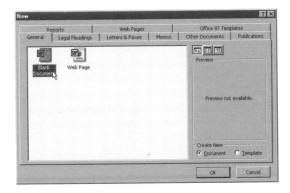

2 SAVING A FILE
• Drop down the File menu from the menu bar. Click on Save.

• If the file has already been saved, the Save command will simply save the new version and you may continue typing. If you are saving the file for the first time, the Save As dialog box appears and you can assign the document a name and a location.

3 OPENING A FILE

• Drop down the File menu from the menu bar. Click on Open. The Open dialog box appears.

• The Open dialog box shows the files you have already saved. Click on the file you want and then click on Open.

• The file opens and you may begin working on it.

4 CLOSING A FILE

• You usually close a document when you have finished working on it. Drop down the File menu and click on Close.

• If you have not saved your text, or if you have changed it since you last saved, you are asked if you want to save the file.

• Click on Yes if you have forgotten to save your work. Click on No if you're absolutely sure that you don't want to save either the document or the changes you have made since you last saved. If in doubt, click on Cancel and return to the document.

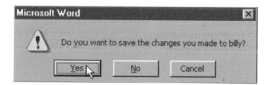

5 SAVING THE FILE TO FLOPPY DISK

• Click on Save As in the File menu to open the Save As dialog box.

• Drop down the Save In menu in the dialog box.

• Click on 3½ Floppy (A:) in the Save In menu.

• Click OK and your file is saved to the floppy disk.

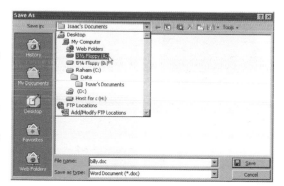

PRINTING

You will want your letter to appear on paper looking as neat as possible. Word has features that let you preview the printout of your letter, make improvements, and finally print your letter.

PRINT PREVIEW

Print Preview lets you see how the printed version of your letter will appear. This is done by showing each page as a scaled-down version of the specified paper size – usually 8½ x 11. The changes you can make in Print Preview include adjusting the margins, but it's not possible to edit the text when previewing. You can preview one page at a time or view several pages at once. Seeing more than one page lets you compare how they look and see how your changes affect your letter.

1 PREVIEW YOUR TEXT

• Open a file that you want to print out.

• Go to the top of the text with the insertion point ⌐.

• Click on File in the Menu bar and click on Print Preview in the File drop-down menu.

• Your screen now shows a print preview of your letter.

⌐ Insertion
12 point

2 SHOWING MULTIPLE PAGES

• If your letter has more than one page, you may want to see them all on one screen. Look at the Print Preview toolbar (now the only toolbar at the top of the screen). There is a rounded box containing four small rectangles (shown at right). This is the Multiple pages icon.

• Click on the Multiple Pages icon, a menu of gray pages appears.

• Move the mouse pointer over the menu to choose

how many pages you want to view. In the example shown, "1 x 2" pages is selected. The first number is the number of rows in which your pages appear, the second number is the number of pages to be shown. The maximum is 3 x 8, which is selected by holding down the left mouse button and moving the mouse pointer right.

• Release the mouse button over the required display.

• You can now see how your letter will appear on the printed page.

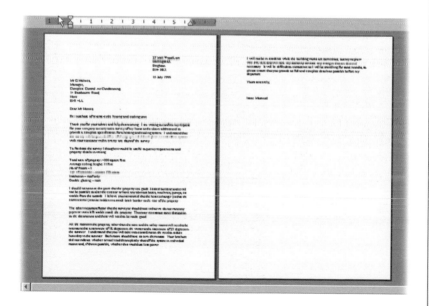

3 PAGE SETUP

● You may want to improve the look of your letter. Perhaps there is not enough room between the text and the edge of the paper. Or maybe a couple of lines spill onto a new page that could fit on the previous page. Both these problems can be solved by changing the margins.

● Begin by dropping down the File menu and click on Page Setup.

● The Page Setup dialog box appears.

4 CHANGING THE MARGINS

● There are four boxes in the Page Setup dialog box to control the top, bottom, left, and right margins.

● You can increase or decrease the margins by increments of one-tenth of an inch by clicking the up and down arrow buttons to the right of each margin control box. Or click inside a box to enter a size.

● When you have selected the margin sizes, click the OK box to see your results.

● When you are satisfied with your changes, click on Close in the Print Preview toolbar to return to the normal view of your letter.

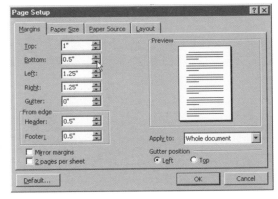

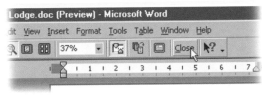

PRINTING YOUR LETTER

The actual process of printing out your letter is very simple. The Print Preview feature makes it unnecessary to print a number of draft versions of your letter

because you now know how it will appear on the page. All that is left to do now is to use the very simple Print command to produce a hard copy of your letter.

1 THE PRINT DIALOG BOX

● Drop down the File menu and click on Print to open the Print dialog box.

● You can print selected pages of your letter if you want. Enter the numbers of the pages into the Pages box under Page Range.

● You can also print more than one copy of your letter. Enter the number you want into the Number of Copies box at the right of the Print dialog box.

● Check that your printer is connected to your computer and that it is switched on.

● Click on OK and your letter begins to be printed.

PRINTING QUICKLY

In most cases, you will not need to "customize" your printing because you simply need one copy of all the pages of your letter. Click on the printer icon in the toolbar at the top of the screen. Your letter is printed without using the Print dialog box.

Enter the number of copies required ●

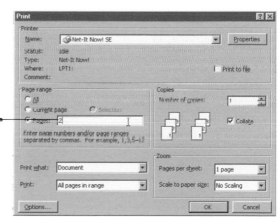

LET WORD HELP

Word has many helpful features including a spelling checker, a grammar checker, a thesaurus, templates on which to base your documents, and wizards that produce customized documents.

SPELLING CHECKER

However good your letter looks on paper, it can be let down by typing errors. Even if your spelling is impeccable it is inevitable that some incorrect keystrokes are made.

Word can check your spelling for you as you type, or you can have Word check the spelling of your whole document when you've finished writing it.

1 CHECKING AS YOU TYPE

● Try typing a deliberate mistake into your letter.
● A wavy red line appears below the incorrect word.
● Move the mouse pointer over the word containing the error and click with the right mouse button (right click). A pop up menu appears near the word.
● Word lists alternative words that you could have intended to type instead of the mistake. Left-click on the correct word.

Dear Margaret

Thanks for your leter|

Thanks for your letter

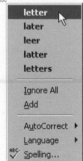

letter
later
leer
latter
letters
I̲gnore All
A̲dd
Au̲toCorrect ▶
L̲anguage ▶
Spelling...

• The mistake is replaced by the correct word and the pop up closes.

Dear Margaret

Thanks for your letter|

2 ADDING WORDS

• Now type something that is correct but obscure which the spelling checker is unlikely to recognize, such as a foreign word or an unusual name.

• The word, though not a mistake, is underlined by the wavy red line.

• Right click the word. The menu drops down.

• Click on Add. The spelling checker adds the word to its dictionary and will no longer underline the word as a "mistake."

• The wavy red line disappears because the spelling is now accepted as being correct.

Dear Margaret

Thanks for your letter. I've made some calls to but so far no luck. C'est la vie.|

Thanks for your letter. I've made some calls to but so far no luck. C'est la vie.

Chest
Crest
Chests
Crests
Less

Ignore All
Add

AutoCorrect ▶
Language ▶
Spelling...

Dear Margaret

Thanks for your letter. I've made some calls to but so far no luck. C'est la vie.

GRAMMAR CHECKER

Word's automatic grammar checker works very much like the spelling checker. The obvious difference is that Word marks what it believes to be grammatical errors with a wavy green line, not a red line. The grammar checker cannot offer perfect advice due to the complexities of English. So accept its suggestions carefully.

CORRECTING GRAMMAR

• Word has detected a clumsy sentence structure.
• Right-click the sentence and a menu pops up.
• Choose the suggestion or click on About this Sentence to have the problem explained. Click on Ignore if you think the grammar checker is itself making a mistake.
• If you click on About this Sentence, the office assistant, which can be switched on by using the Help menu, pops up and explains what Word thinks is the problem.
• Click with the mouse button away from the advice to close the panel.

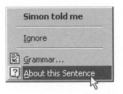

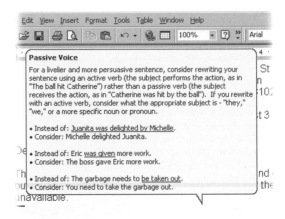

● Right-click the sentence again to display the pop up menu and click on the suggested correction.

r. I've made some calls to try to find out what you st la vie. I was told by Simon that the information

Simon told me

Ignore

Grammar...

About this Sentence

r. I've made some calls to try to find out what you st la vie. Simon told me that the information is

The grammar of the sentence has been revised

THESAURUS

You may want to find an alternative word to express what you mean. The thesaurus feature in Word lists possible words in the same way as the paper based thesaurus except that it works directly on the word for which you require a synonym.

SYNONYMS

● Place the insertion point in the word for which you want to find a synonym.
● Drop down the Tools menu from the menu bar. Click on Language.
● A submenu appears, click on Thesaurus.

Thanks for your letter. I've made some calls to but so far no luck. C'est la vie. Simon told me unavailable. It's annoying

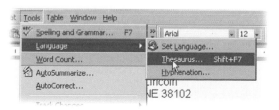

• The Thesaurus dialog box appears. Synonyms are listed on the right-hand side.

• Click on a synonym. It appears in the Replace with Synonym box.

• Click on the Replace button.

• The word is replaced with the synonym.

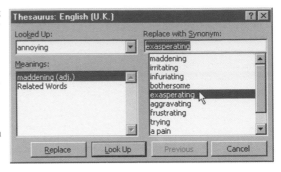

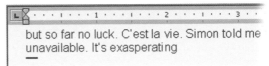

CHECKING AFTER YOU HAVE FINISHED TYPING

Some people find that having Word checking their spelling and grammar as they type is distracting and intrusive. If you would prefer not to have the wavy red and green underlines appearing below your text, you can turn these functions off.

1 TURNING OFF CHECKING

• To turn off the spelling checker while you type, drop down the Tools menu from the toolbar.

• Click on Options and the Options dialog box opens on screen.

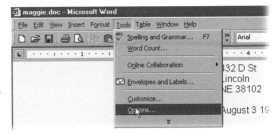

• There are a number of tabs at the top of the Options dialog box for altering different aspects of Word. Click on the Spelling & Grammar tab to display the available options under Spelling and Grammar.

• Click once in the Check spelling as you type tick box. The tick disappears

• Click on the OK button. Word will now no longer check your spelling as you type. You can still, however, check the spelling of all the text in one pass, after you have finished typing.

• If you wish to stop Word checking the grammar, click once in the Check grammar as you type tick box. The tick disappears and the grammar checker is turned off.

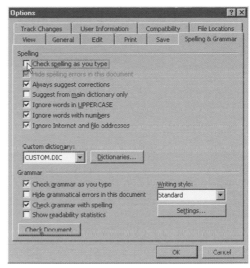

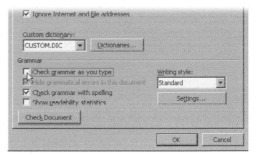

2 CHECKING THE DOCUMENT

● Drop down the Tools menu from the menu bar.

● Click on Spelling and Grammar from the Tools menu. Word will work through your document with the Spelling and Grammar dialog box, prompting you at every error that is found.

● If you want to accept a suggested spelling, click on the correct one from the Suggestions box and click on the Change button.

● If you want to correct the error yourself, click inside the Not in Dictionary box and position the insertion point over the error. Make the text correction yourself by using the keyboard and click on the Change button.

● If you don't think that there is an error, click on the Ignore button.

● Word moves on to the next error in your text until it can find no more and the information box appears telling you that the check is complete. Click on OK.

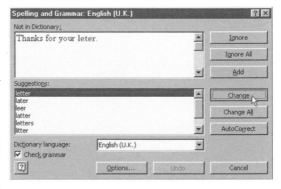

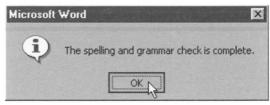

TEMPLATES

Usually when you come to create a new file, either you work from the blank file that Word creates when it is launched, or you create a new blank file by choosing the Blank Document option from the New dialog box. This time, you can save yourself some of the work involved in laying out a document by creating a preformatted letter and filling in the blanks. As an example of this, follow the steps below to create a letter using the Elegant Letter template.

1 CREATE A NEW FILE

• Drop down the File menu and click on New.
• In the New dialog box click on the Letters & Faxes tab and click on the icon labeled Elegant Letter.
• Click on OK.

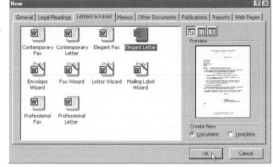

2 FILLING IN THE BLANKS

• Your new file will now be open on the screen.
• Click on the box at the top of the letter marked Click here and type in your company's name. The box itself is not printed out - it's only to show you the boundaries of where you can type.

• Click on the line of text that reads Click here and type recipient's address. You can begin typing the recipient's address – the line of text vanishes when you begin typing.

13 Augu

[Click **here** and type recipient's address] I

Dear Sir or Madam:

Type your letter here. For more details on modifying this letter letter, use the Window menu.

Sincerely,

• Using the insertion point or the mouse pointer, select the text of the paragraph that is already in place and begin typing. The old text disappears as you begin to start typing.

13 Augu

[Click **here** and type recipient's address]

Dear Sir or Madam:

Type your letter here. For more details on modifying this letter letter, use the Window menu. I

Sincerely,

• Add your name and job title over the lines of text at the end of the letter. Just click in these lines to select them, and start typing.

Sincerely,

[Click **here** and type your name] I
[Click **here** and type job title]

• Your address goes at the foot of the Elegant Letter. Scroll down the page and add your address into the address box.

• You have now created a letter using the Elegant Letter template.

|STREET ADDRESS| · |CITY/STATE| · |ZIP/POSTAL CODE|
PHONE· |PHONE NUMBER| · FAX· |FAX NUMBER|

WIZARDS

Wizards are a simple way of producing formatted letters quickly. There is no need to type names and addresses directly into the letter – Word uses dialog boxes for you to supply the information and then adds this to the letter. You can create the same letter using the Letter Wizard that you did using the template.

1 STARTING THE WIZARD

- Drop down the File menu and click on New as usual.
- Click the Letters & Faxes tab and click on the icon marked Letter Wizard.
- Click on the OK button.
- A small dialog box appears along with the office assistant.
- Click on Send one letter.

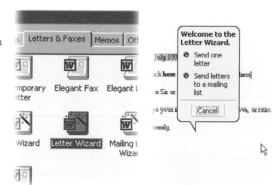

2 LETTER FORMAT

- The Letter Wizard dialog box opens. There are four steps in the Letter Wizard the first is Letter Format.
- Drop down the Choose a page design menu and choose the one you want. You will notice that Elegant Letter, the template we used earlier in this section, is one of the designs.
- Drop down the Letter Style menu and choose from Full Block (no

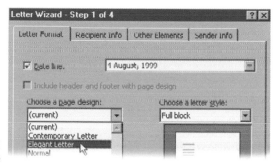

indents), Modified Block (some indenting), or Semi-Block (full, with stylish first line indents).
- Click on the Next button to go to the next section.

3 RECIPIENT'S INFORMATION

- The Letter Wizard dialog box now shows the Recipient Info step.
- Enter the recipient's name and address in the relevant text boxes.
- Choose a salutation from the drop-down menu under Salutation, or type in your own.
- Click on the Next button.

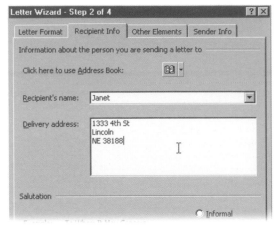

4 OTHER ELEMENTS

- The Letter Wizard dialog box now shows the Other Elements step.
- If you want to include a reference line, click on the check box to the left of Reference Line. A tick will appear in the box. You can now drop down the Reference Line menu and use the available options.
- Do the same for any other features you want: Mailing Instruction, Attention, Subject.
- If you wish to send a courtesy copy, insert the details into the boxes at the foot of the dialog box.
- Click on the Next button.

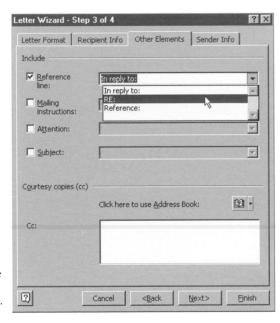

5 SENDER INFORMATION

- The last step of the Letter Wizard dialog box is the Sender Info step.
- Type your name into the Sender's name box.
- Type your address into the Return address box.
- Select a closing from the Complimentary closing drop-down menu – or type your own into the box.
- Click on Finish to allow the Letter Wizard to create your document.

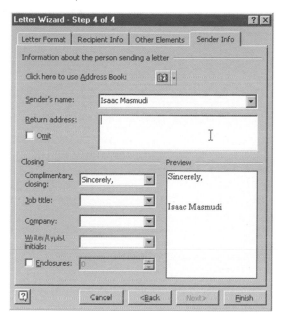

6 START TYPING

- The Letter Wizard dialog box vanishes. The office assistant appears and asks you if you want to do any more to your letter.
- Make a selection or click on Cancel.
- Your letter is ready. Everything is in place except the paragraphs of main text.
- Start typing as with the Elegant Letter template.

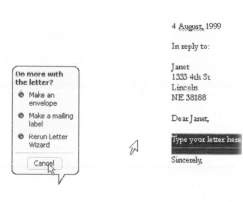

MAIL MERGE

Mail merge is a way of sending personalized letters to a number of people. Although more often used by business, mail merge is useful for telling people about the large events in our lives.

MAIN DOCUMENTS AND DATA SOURCES

So far you have only been working with letters to individual recipients. You may however wish to create a letter to be sent to a number of people – for instance, to notify all your friends that you have moved. You could produce a letter addressed to one person, print it out, change the recipient's name and address, print out the new letter to the next person, and so on. This would however be a very tedious and time-consuming process. To save you this trouble you can use a feature called Mail Merge. This allows you to create a standard letter and a list of names and addresses. The letter and the list are then merged to create personalized letters to everyone in the list. The standard letter is called a Main Document – the list is called a Data Source. Let's start by creating a Main Document from scratch.

1 CREATE A MAIN DOCUMENT
- Drop down the Tools menu and click on the Mail Merge option.
- The Mail Merge Helper dialog box opens.
- Click on the Create button under Main Document.

• A menu drops down.
Click on Form Letters at
the top of the menu.
• A dialog box opens. Click
on New Main Document.
• A blank document will
appear under the Mail
Merge Helper dialog box.
This is your Main
Document.

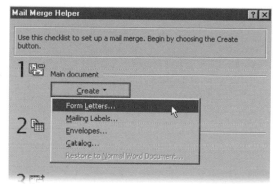

2 CREATE A DATA SOURCE

• Before working on your
new Master Document, you
need to create a structure
for your data. You need a
Data Source to do this.
• Click on the Get Data
button under Data Source
in the Mail Merge Helper
dialog box.
• Click on Create Data
Source in the menu

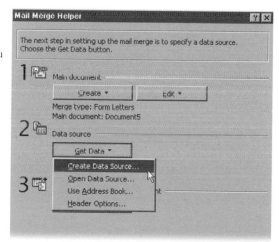

• The Create Data Source dialog box opens.

• The list shows the fields (see Fields and Records below) that are going to make up the Data Source.

• You won't need all the fields. You can remove the fields with the Remove Field Name button. Add new ones by typing a new field name into the Field name box and clicking on Add Field Name.

• Remove all the fields except Address1, Address2, City, and Postcode.

• Now type Name into the Field name box. Click on the Add Field Name button. You have created a new field called Name.

• Your list of fields should appear as shown at right.

• Now click on OK.

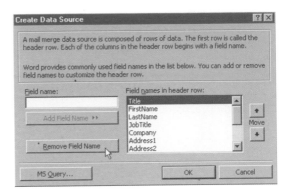

FIELDS AND RECORDS

Each kind of data in the Master Document that is attached to the Data Source (such as the recipient's names, or each line of their addresses) is called a field. Fields are what link the Master Document to the Data Source. The actual data in the fields – such as in the Name field, James, Mr. Doncaster, Mum & Dad – are called records.

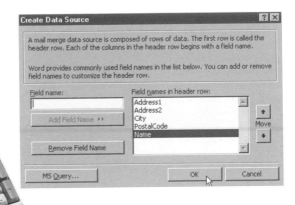

• The Save As dialog box opens. Type List in the File Name box and click the Save button.
• You have now created a Data Source.
• A dialog box will appear. Click on Edit Data Source.

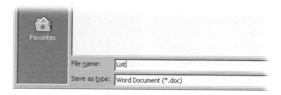

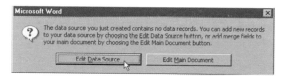

3 ENTER RECORDS

• The Data Form dialog box opens and you can edit the Data Source.
• Type the name and address of your first recipient into the boxes in the dialog box.
• When you have finished with the first recipient, move to a fresh record by clicking the Add New button. The field boxes empty and you are ready to type in a new record.
• Add as many records as you want. You can go back to your old records and correct them with the buttons at the foot of the dialog box.
• When you have finished entering all the records that you wish to include, click on OK.

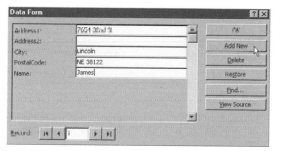

4 INSERT MERGE FIELDS

• The Data Form dialog box closes. You will now see the Main Document.

• Type in your own address and the date.

• Instead of typing the first line of the recipient's address, click on the Insert Merge Field button on the Mail Merge toolbar at the top of the screen.

• A menu drops down. Click on Address1.

• The field will appear in the letter as <<Address1>>. Don't worry, it won't print out like this – it is a way of showing you the structure of your Main Document before it is merged with the Data Source.

• Add the remainder of the address by entering one line in each field.

• Type Dear, leave a space, and add the Name field from the Insert Merge Field drop-down menu.

• Finish your letter in the normal way.

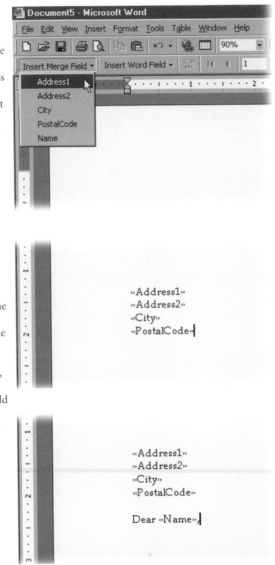

5 READY TO MERGE

• Check your Main Document. It should look something like the document shown at right.

•To make sure you are ready to print your mail merge, click on the View Merged Data button on the Mail Merge toolbar at the top of the screen.

•This shows your letter as it will go out to each person. The arrow buttons on the Mail Merge toolbar allow you to move through different records.

«Address1»
«Address2»
«City»
«PostalCode»

Dear «Name»,

Just a quick note to let you kn the launch of Masmudi Enterp

We would love to see you the come.

Many thanks

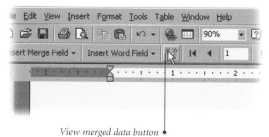

View merged data button •

Next record button •

6 CHECK YOUR MAIL MERGE

• With the View Merged Data button down (it will stay down until you click it again – don't try to hold it down with the mouse), you will be able to see the different versions of the same letter that are going out to different recipients.

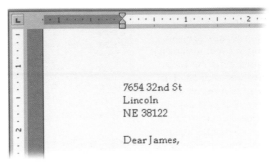

7654 32nd St
Lincoln
NE 38122

Dear James,

• Each letter displays the same basic text, but the details of the individual recipient's are different.

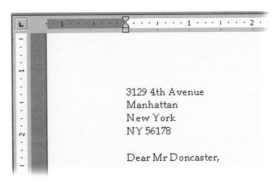

3129 4th Avenue
Manhattan
New York
NY 56178

Dear Mr Doncaster,

• When you have finished viewing, click on the View Merged Data button again to return to normal view of the Main Document.

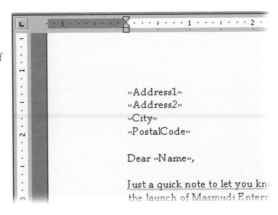

«Address1»
«Address2»
«City»
«PostalCode»

Dear «Name»,

Just a quick note to let you kno
the launch of Masmudi Enterp

7 PRINT MERGE

• You are now ready to print out your mail merge.
• Drop down the Tools menu and click on Mail Merge to bring up the Mail Merge Helper dialog box.
• Click the Merge button in the Mail Merge Helper dialog box. The Merge dialog box opens.
• Drop down the Merge To menu with the small down arrow box at the side of the Merge To box.
• Click on Printer.
• The Merge To box now contains the word Printer.
• Click on Merge. The Print dialog box opens.
• Click on OK.
• All copies of the letter, each personalized for the individual recipient, will now be printed.

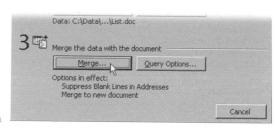

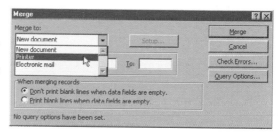

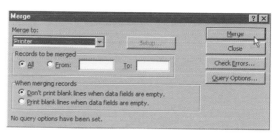

8 SAVING THE FILES

Once you have finished with your mail merge, close down the file as normal (click on Close from the File menu). You will be prompted with a dialog box asking you if you want to save the changes to your Data Source. Click on Yes to save your current data. Then, if you have made any changes to the Main Document, you will be asked if you want to save the changes, as normal. Click on Yes if you want to keep the changes.

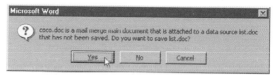

GLOSSARY

ALIGNMENT
In word processing, this refers to the side of the text that is aligned in a straight vertical line along one side (for instance, left-aligned text is straight on the left side and the ends of the lines are ragged on the right).

BLOCK (OF TEXT)
A selected portion of the text, highlighted in white letters on a black 'block' on the screen.

COPY
To copy part of the text so that the same piece of text can be 'pasted' into a new position (in the same document or another document) without removing the original piece of text.

CUT
To remove a block of text, in order to remove it permanently or to 'paste' into a new position (in the same document or another document).

DATA SOURCE
In a mail merge, the list containing the data that will fill in the blanks in the main document.

DIALOG BOX
A rectangle that appears on the screen and prompts you for a reply, usually with buttons, e.g. OK or Cancel.

DOCUMENT
A file containing user data, such as text written in Word.

FIELD
In a mail merge, a variable part of the text, e.g. the name in "Dear <<Name>>"

FILE
A discrete piece of data stored on the computer.

FOLDER
A folder stores files and other folders, to keep files organized.

FONT
The typeface in which text appears on screen and when it is printed out.

INDENT
The indent shifts part of the text, or just the first line in every paragraph, across the screen.

INSERTION POINT
A blinking upright line on the screen. As you type, text appears at the insertion point.

JUSTIFIED TEXT
Text which is aligned to both left and right sides, so there is no ragged edge either side.

MAIL MERGE
A way of combining a list of data for different people with a set letter, to send a single letter to many people at once.

MAIN DOCUMENT
In a mail merge, the master document is the bulk of the text with blanks (fields) to be filled with records from the data source.

MARGIN
The distance between the text and the paper edge. There are four margins on a page: top, bottom, left, and right.

PASTE
To put text which has been 'cut' or 'copied' back into the document at the insertion point.

PRINT PREVIEW
A mock-up on the screen of exactly how your text will appear on paper. This allows you to make final changes to the look of your letter without wasting paper.

RECORD
In a mail merge, a record is one entry for a certain field, such as "John" in the "Name" field.

RULER
Indicators at the top and left of the screen, with marks in inches or centimeters like a real ruler. Rulers also show the indents and margins of the text.

SCROLL
To scroll is to move up or down the document.

SCROLL BARS
Bars at the foot and the right of the screen that can be used to scroll around the document. The vertical one (on the right) is the more useful.

TEMPLATE
Blank files with the formatting (not the text) already set up for a particular style of document, e.g. an invoice or a formal business letter.

WIZARD
Interactive sequences that ask you questions and then set up a new file for you.

INDEX

A

adding words
  dictionary 51
  text 17
address
  indent 30–1
  typing 12–13
  see also mail merge
alignment 34–5

BC

bold type 36, 38
centering text 35
checking
  mail merge 68
  spelling and grammar 50–3,
    54–6
copying text 28
corrections
  spelling 50–1
  typing errors 14–16
cursor *see* insertion point
customizing
  printing requirements 49
  toolbars 11
cut and paste 27–8

DEF

data source, mail merge 63–4
dictionary 51
double spacing 40–1
drag and drop 29
errors, correction 14–16
fields 64
files 42–5
floppy disks 43
folders 44–5
fonts 36–9
formatting 30–41
  fonts 36–9
  layout 30–5
  line spacing 40–1
  templates 57–8
  toolbar 8–9
  wizards 59–61
formatting marks 15

GHI

grammar 52–3, 54–6
green line 52
hanging indent 33
indents 30–3
inserting text 17
insertion point 12
  positioning 22–4
italics 36, 39

JKL

justified text 34–5
keyboard
  moving insertion point 22–3
  selecting text 24–5
layout 30–5
letter wizard 59–61
lines
  selecting 26
  spacing 40–1
  red/green 50–2

M

mail merge
  checking 68
  main document 62–3, 66–7
  names and addresses 63–5
  printing 69
margins 48
menu bar 8
mouse
  moving insertion point 23–4
  selecting text 25
moving text 27–9
multiple copies, printing 49
multiple pages, print preview
  46–7

NO

names and addresses, mail
  merge 63–4
new page 19
opening files 43
options, spelling and grammar
  54–5

PQR

pages
  new 19
  preview 46–7
  printing 49
  setup 48
paragraphs
  creating 13, 18–19
  indenting 32–3
personalized letters
  see mail merge
positioning insertion point
  22–3
pre-formatted letters 57–8
printing
  dialog box 21, 49
  mail merge 69
  page setup 48
  preview 46–7
records 64–5
red line 50–1
ruler 30

S

saving
  floppy disk 43
  folders 45
  letters 20, 42
  mail merge 69
scrolling 23
selecting
  pages to print 49
  text 24–6
sentence structure 52–3
shortcuts, formatting 36
size, font 37
spacing, lines 40–1
spelling check
  at end 54–6
  during typing 50–1
storing *see* saving
styles
  fonts 38–9
  letters 57–61
synonyms 53–4

T

templates 57–8
text 22–9
  alignment 34–5
  centering 35
  copying 28
  fonts 36–9
  indenting 30–3
  inserting 17
  moving 27–9
  selecting 24–6

thesaurus 53–4
toolbars, Word 9–11
typeface 36–9

U

underlining
  font style 36, 39
  green 52
  red 50–1

VW

wizards 59–61
Word
  capabilities 6
  launching 7
  toolbars 9–11
  window 8–9

ACKNOWLEDGMENTS

PUBLISHER'S ACKNOWLEDGMENTS
Dorling Kindersley would like to thank the following:
Paul Mattock of APM, Brighton, for commissioned photography.
Microsoft Corporation for permission to reproduce screens
from within Microsoft® Word 2000.

Every effort has been made to trace the copyright holders.
The publisher apologizes for any unintentional omissions and would be pleased,
in such cases, to place an acknowledgment in future editions of this book.